Do You Love Me?

Learning to Read from the Bible Series

Primers

MAY I HELP YOU?
DO YOU KNOW MY FRIEND?
DO YOU LOVE ME?
WILL YOU COME WITH ME?

Readers

GOD IS MY HELPER
GOD IS MY FRIEND
JESUS IS MY TEACHER
JESUS IS MY GUIDE

Learning to read · from the Bible ·

Do You Love Me?

By V. Gilbert Beers
Illustrated by Jan M. Jones

ZONDERVAN
PUBLISHING HOUSE OF THE ZONDERVAN CORPORATION
GRAND RAPIDS, MICHIGAN 49506

What's in This Book

A Word to Parents and Teachers

Do You Love Me?

Did You Come to Love Me?	Luke 2:1-20
Do You Love the Children?	Mark 10:13-16
Do You Love Poor People?	Luke 18:35-43
How Much Do You Love Me?	Luke 23:33-37, 47

What Will You Do for Me?

Will You Show Me What to Do?	I Kings 3:16-28
Will You Give Me Food to Eat?	I Kings 17:1-6
Will You Help Me Find Your Home?	Luke 15:3-7

Do You Love Me?

© 1976 by V. Gilbert Beers

Library of Congress Catalog Card Number: 76-20328

Printed in the United States of America.

This Is My Family

Ruth's New Family   The Book of Ruth

Samuel Gets a New Home

                   1 Samuel 1:9-28; 2:11,18-21

Jesus' Happy Family   Luke 2:51-52

What These Stories Teach

Basic Word List

New Word List

A Word to Parents and Teachers

This book is part of the "Learning to Read from the Bible" Series. Basic words which your child reads have come from standard word lists and school reading programs at the primer level. No more than five new words are introduced with each story.

All reading material for the child is vocabulary controlled. Each word which the child reads comes from the basic word list, except for the new words listed for each story.

Since word lists are compatible with school reading programs, your child should find it comfortable to use this book as supplementary reading for his school primer. You will also find it helpful for church schools, home devotions and Bible reading, and Christian day schools. In addition, your child will find a special delight in reading this book himself, for he will sense that special joy of "Learning to Read from the Bible."

V. GILBERT BEERS

Do You
Love Me?

Did You Come
to Love Me?

"You can not stay here,"
the man said.

"I have all the people I
can take."

"But where can we sleep?"
Joseph asked.

"Mary is going to have a baby."

The man looked at his animals.

"You may sleep with them," he said.

"It is all I have."

So Mary and Joseph went
to sleep with the animals.
That night Mary had a
little baby.

"We know," said Mary and
Joseph.

"This baby is God's Son.
He has come to love us. And
He has come to help us love
God."

Something to Know

Jesus   Mary

God   Joseph

sleep

Something to Ask

1. Who was this little baby?

2. Why did He come?

3. Does Jesus love you?

4. Do you love Jesus?

5. How can you show Him that you love Him?

Something to Do

How do you show Jesus that
you love Him? What would
tell Him that?

Do You Love
the Children?

"What do you want?" some
of Jesus' friends asked.
"We want to have our
children see Jesus," said
the mothers and fathers.

"You can not do that," said Jesus' friends.

"Why not?" asked the mothers and fathers.

"Jesus has too many things to do," said His friends.

"That's why!"

Then Jesus came to them.
"What is it?" He asked.
"Your friends will not
let our children see You,"
said the mothers and fathers.
"We told them You are
doing other things," said
His friends.

"Do not tell the children to stay away from Me," said Jesus.

"They show others how to come to Me."

Then Jesus had the children
come to see Him.

He told them many things.

He told them about God.

He told them about His
home in heaven.

And He told them how God
loved them.

"Do You love us, too?" the children asked.

"Yes," said Jesus.

"And I want you to love Me."

Something to Know

heaven   which

Something to Ask

1. Did Jesus make the children go away?

2. Why did He let them come to Him?

3. Does Jesus love children?

4. What can you do for Jesus?

Something to Do

Which kind of children does Jesus love?

To Parents and Teachers: Talk with your child about the different children in the picture above. Does Jesus love one more than the others? Why not? Help your child to think about this in his own life. Should he love some children more than others?

Do You Love Poor People?

One day Jesus was going into a town.

A poor man sat by the road.

He wanted someone to help him.

The man could not see.

He could not work.

He could not get food to eat.

Then Jesus came by.

"Help me," he said to
Jesus.

"Help me! Help me! Help
me!"

"Stop that!" some people
said.

But the man did not stop.

"Have him come here," said Jesus.

So some men helped him come to Jesus.

"What do you want?" Jesus asked.

"I want to see," said the man.

"Then you will see," said Jesus.

At once the man could see.

He was so happy.

He could see trees.

He could see people.

And he could see Jesus.

"Thank You! Thank You!"

the man said.

Then the man went with Jesus to help Him do His work.

He knew that Jesus loved him very much.

And he loved Jesus very much, too.

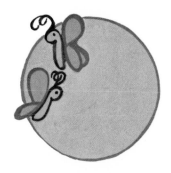

Something to Know

once   poor

Something to Ask

1. What did the poor man want?

2. What did Jesus do for him?

3. Does Jesus love poor people?

4. How do you know?

5. Do you love poor people, too?

6. What can you do for them?

Then the man went with Jesus to help Him do His work.

He knew that Jesus loved him very much.

And he loved Jesus very much, too.

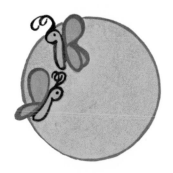

Something to Know

once   poor

Something to Ask

1. What did the poor man want?

2. What did Jesus do for him?

3. Does Jesus love poor people?

4. How do you know?

5. Do you love poor people, too?

6. What can you do for them?

Something to Do

Which of these will help you most?

Would you be poor without them?

How Much
Do You Love Me?

"Nail that Man to the cross!" someone said.
The men nailed Jesus to the cross.

Then they watched Him die.

Jesus had not hurt these men.

But they were hurting Him.

Then Jesus talked to God about these men.

"Don't hurt them for hurting Me," He said.

These people had not
seen a man like this.
They were hurting Him.
But He was loving them.
"That Man is God's Son,"
said one of them.

When Jesus died
on the cross, He
showed how much
He loved them.
He showed
how much He
loves you and me.
Does Jesus love
us very much?

He loved us so much that
He died to help us come to
God.

Can He love us any more
than that?

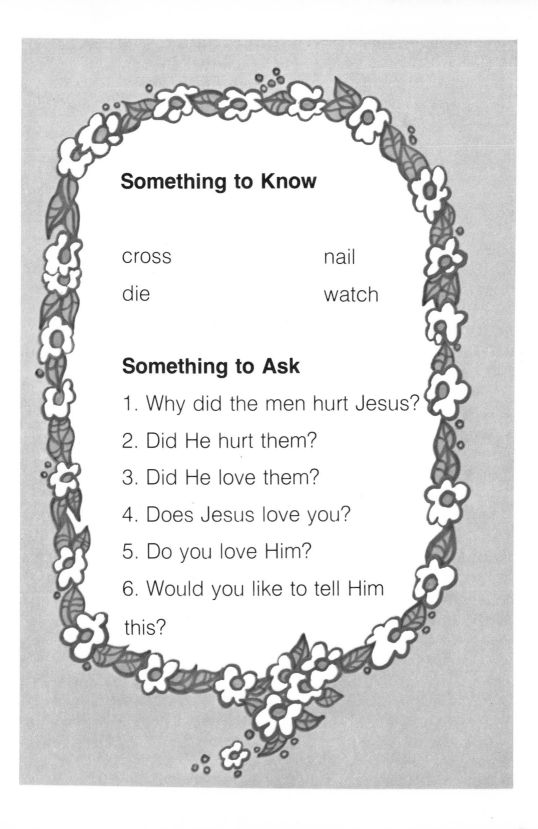

Something to Know

cross   nail

die   watch

Something to Ask

1. Why did the men hurt Jesus?

2. Did He hurt them?

3. Did He love them?

4. Does Jesus love you?

5. Do you love Him?

6. Would you like to tell Him

this?

Something to Do

What can you do with these for Jesus?

How can you say "I love You"?

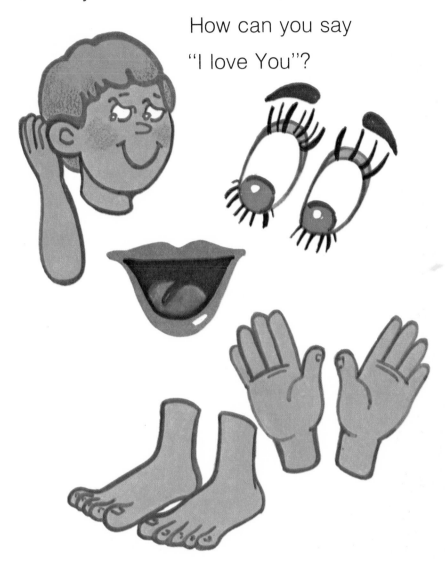

To Parents and Teachers: Talk with your child about the ways he can use his eyes, ears, mouth, hands, and feet to tell his love to Jesus. Remind him of such things as singing, praying, telling others about Jesus, listening to Bible stories, putting money in the offering, and many others.

What Will You Do
for Me?

Will You Show Me What to Do?

"Long live King Solomon," the people said.

Solomon was the new king.

He was a very wise king.
He had asked God to make him wise.

One day some women
came with a baby.

"That is my baby,"
said one.

"No, it is my baby,"
said the other.

Solomon did not know
who was the mother.

"Cut the baby in two,"
said Solomon.

"Give some of it to each
woman."

NO!

said the mother.

YES!

said the other
woman.

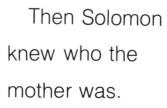

Then Solomon
knew who the
mother was.

"Give the baby to
that woman," he said.
"How wise our king
is," said the people.
"Thank You, God, for
showing me what to do,"
said King Solomon.

Something to Know

Solomon   wise

cut   two

each

Something to Ask

1. Why did Solomon know
what to do?
2. What did he do to
show that he was wise?
3. Do you want someone to
help you know what to do?
4. Who can help you most?
5. Will you ask Him?

Something to Do

What would God want you to do?

this?   or   that?

To Parents and Teachers: Talk about the kinds of things which please God and those which displease Him. Suggest to your child that he ask "What would God want me to do?" whenever he is uncertain about doing something. He may also ask "What would Jesus do?"

Will You Give Me
Food to Eat?

Elijah had to run away.

He had told the king what God said.

But the king did not like what God said.

He did not like to hear how bad he was.

So the king wanted to
kill Elijah.
"You must hide from the
king," God said.

"Where?"
asked Elijah.
"I will show you,"
God said.
God showed Elijah a
little river.

"But what will I eat?"

Elijah asked.

There was no food at

the river.

Then God sent food
each day for Elijah.
He sent birds with
Elijah's food.
Now Elijah had good
food to eat.

God gave it to him each day.

"Thank You," Elijah said.

"Thank You for giving me good food to eat."

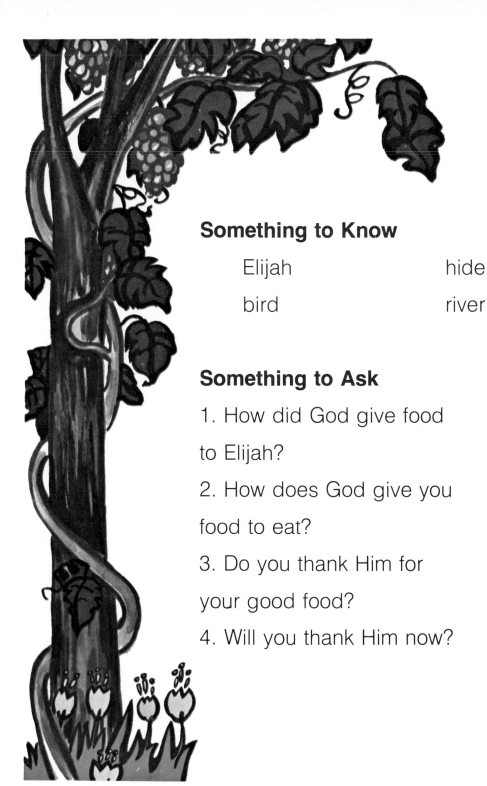

Something to Know

Elijah   hide

bird   river

Something to Ask

1. How did God give food
to Elijah?
2. How does God give you
food to eat?
3. Do you thank Him for
your good food?
4. Will you thank Him now?

Something to Do

Which food did God give you?

To Parents and Teachers: Talk with your child about the different foods here and how we get them. Remind him of the way God provides each kind, even the foods you buy in cans and boxes. Talk about man's part in preparing these foods and God's part in their growth.

Will You Help Me
Find Your Home?

One day Jesus told His
friends about a sheep.
It was a sheep that
ran away.

The sheep went far
away from the others.

It could not find
the way home.

Then the shepherd
saw that his sheep was
gone.

He loved his sheep.
He wanted to find it.

So he went away from
the others.
He went far away from
home.

He looked and looked
for his sheep.
Then he found it.
The shepherd took the
sheep into his arms.

Then he took that sheep
to his home.

Jesus said that the
sheep was like us.
We are far away from
God.

But Jesus came.
He loves us.
And He helps us find
the way to God's home in
heaven.

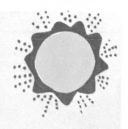

Something to Know

sheep   shepherd

found   arm

Something to Ask

1. Why did the shepherd look for his sheep?

2. Why does Jesus want to help you come to God?

3. Do you want to live in God's home in heaven some day?

4. Have you asked Jesus to show you His way?

5. Will you do that now?

Something to Do

How can you find the way
to God's home in heaven?

look for it
your way

go where your
friends tell you

ask Jesus
to show you

This Is
My Family

Ruth's New Family

"I am going home," Naomi said.

"I am going back to my people."

Many things had hurt Naomi. Her husband had died. Her boys had died.

Now she wanted to go back to her home.

"I will go with you," said Ruth.

So Ruth went back with Naomi to her people.

But Ruth had
to get food
for them to eat.
There was no
other one to
do it.

One day Ruth saw a good man.

His name was Boaz.

Boaz loved Ruth.

Ruth loved Boaz.

"May I be your husband?"

Boaz asked Ruth.

Ruth was very happy.

She was happy to have Boaz
for her husband.

"Boaz will take care of
Naomi and me," she said.

"And he will
love me, too."

After a time, Ruth and Boaz
had a baby boy.
They were a very, very
happy family.

Something to Know

family   Naomi

husband   Ruth

Boaz

Something to Ask

1. Why was Ruth happy?
2. What can make a family happy?
3. Do you have a happy family?
4. What can you do to help your family?
5. Will this make you happy, too?

Something to Do

What is a family? Do these
things make a family?

To Parents and Teachers: Talk with your child about the true meaning of a family. Do houses and cars and things make a family? What is most important in a family? Talk about the things you can do to make your family happy. Talk about the things your family can do for God.

Samuel Gets a New Home

"Please help me," Hannah asked God.

"Help me get a baby boy." Hannah wanted a baby so much.

"If You give me a little boy, he will do Your work," said Hannah.

One day God sent a baby
boy to Hannah.
He was called Samuel.
Hannah was so happy.

"I will give
him to God,"
she said.
"I will do
what I said I
would."

When the boy Samuel was bigger, Hannah took him to God's house.

"Will you help my boy do God's work?" she asked.

"Yes," said Eli, the man who took care of God's house.

So Eli helped
Samuel know
about God.
And Samuel
helped Eli
take care of
God's house.

Samuel stayed with Eli at
God's house.

Hannah took
him many good
things.

Samuel loved his mother.
He loved Eli, too.
But best of all, he loved
God.
And Samuel loved his new
home, for he worked for God
there.

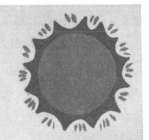

Something to Know

care   Eli

Samuel   Hannah

Something to Ask

1. Where did Samuel live?

2. Why did he live there?

3. Why did Samuel love his
new home?

4. How can you help God do
His work?

Something to Do

When can you talk to God?

When should you talk to God?

To Parents and Teachers: Help your child to see that any time is a good time to talk to God, yet there are special times when we should be sure to talk to Him. We should thank God for food when we eat. We should pray to Him in the morning and evening, in His house, and when we need help.

Jesus' Happy Family

"Will you help me?"
Joseph asked.

Jesus was happy to help
Joseph.

Joseph made many good
things.

He made things from wood.

Joseph was a carpenter.

Jesus was a carpenter, too.

He helped Joseph make

things from wood.

"See what Jesus made?"
Joseph said to Mary.

"Yes," said Mary.

"Jesus is a good carpenter."

Joseph and Mary and Jesus
lived in a little town.

They went to
God's house
in the little town.

They liked to hear God's Word.

They liked to talk to God there.

And they liked to talk to God's people.

"They are a happy family,"
people said.
"They do good work with
wood. But they do good work
for God, too."

Something to Know

carpenter   wood

word

Something to Ask

1. What work did Joseph do?

2. How did Jesus help him?

3. Do good helpers make happy families?

4. Are you a good helper?

5. How can you help your family to be happy?

Something to Do

How can you help your family to be happy?

To Parents and Teachers: Each person in the family has a responsibility to make the whole family happy. Talk about ways that a child can help make the family happy — sharing in the work, reading together, praying for God's help, picking up toys, and being kind to one another.

What These Stories Teach

Each story in this book teaches an important Bible truth, or doctrine. Each story also teaches an important truth about the child's daily living.

These two truths, or objectives, are often so closely related within a story that they may not be obvious to the parent or teacher. All objectives, doctrinal and present-day, are listed here so they may be clearly understood by the parent or teacher.

Story	Doctrinal Objectives	Present-day Objectives
Did You Come to Love Me?	Jesus loves us and wants us to love Him, too.	We should seek ways to show our love to Jesus.
Do You Love the Children?	Jesus loves all children, regardless of age, color, size, shape, or background.	We should remind all children of Jesus' love for them and encourage them to love Him, too.
Do You Love Poor People?	Jesus loves all people, regardless of the amount of money they may have.	We should think about the things that give value to life and consider ourselves rich if we have them.
How Much Do You Love Me?	Jesus loved us enough to die for us so that He could help us get to His home in heaven.	We should seek every way possible to show our love to Jesus. Especially, we should accept Him as our Savior so that we can live with Him in His home.

Will You Show Me What to Do?	God wants us to please Him with the things we do.	We should ask ourselves what God wants us to do, and ask Him, too.
Will You Give Me Food to Eat?	God gives us our food.	We should thank God for all our food.
Will You Help Me Find Your Home?	Jesus knows the way to God's home and wants to help us get there.	We should ask Jesus to be our Guide, leading us to God's home in heaven.
Ruth's New Family	God gives us each other to make a happy family.	We should thank God for each other and recognize that a family is each other, not the things we have.
Samuel Gets a New Home	God wants us to talk to Him at all times, including some special times.	We should remember to talk to God at all times.
Jesus' Happy Family	God has provided ways for a family to be happy together.	We should do our part to make our family happy.

Basic Word List

Most of the 195 words on this basic list have come from standard word lists, school primers, and pre-primers. If your child is reading at the primer level, he should be familiar with most of these words. This will depend, of course, on the specific school reading materials he is using.

With each Bible story you will find the new words which are not found in this basic list. These new words are accumulated into the list of new words which follows.

Variants of a word usually are not considered new words in this book. These include words made by adding s, es, ies, d, ed, ing, er, est, iest, or ly. Thus, calls, called, and calling are not considered new words since call is on the basic word list.

a	by	girl	it	much	sat	the	way
about	call	give	jump	must	saw	their	we
afraid	came	go	kill	my	say	them	well
after	can	gone	kind	new	see	then	went
all	children	good	king	night	seen	there	were
am	come	got	knew	no	sent	these	what
and	could	had	know	not	she	they	when
animal	day	happy	laugh	now	should	thing	where
any	did	has	let	of	show	this	who
are	do	have	lie	on	so	those	why
as	does	he	like	one	some	time	will
ask	down	hear	little	other	someone	to	wind
at	eat	help	live	our	something	told	with
ate	far	her	long	out	son	too	woman
away	fast	here	look	over	soon	took	won
baby	father	him	love	people	stay	town	work
back	find	his	made	play	stop	tree	would
bad	fish	home	make	please	surprise	up	yes
be	food	house	man	put	take	us	you
began	for	how	many	rain	talk	very	your
best	friend	hurt	may	ran	tall	walk	
big	from	I	me	road	tell	want	
boat	fun	in	men	run	than	was	
boy	gave	into	more	sad	thank	wash	
but	get	is	mother	said	that	water	

New Word List

The following is a cumulative list of the thirty-eight new words used in the child's reading material. Words used in the instructions to parents and teachers are not considered for either basic or new word lists.

No more than five new words are used for each story. Often a smaller number is used.

Because these are Bible stories, many of the words are "specialized vocabulary words" relating to the Bible. These words will help to acquaint your beginning reader with Bible names and terms which he should begin to know.

arm	God	river
bird	Hannah	Ruth
Boaz	heaven	Samuel
care	hide	Solomon
carpenter	husband	sheep
cross	Jesus	shepherd
cut	Joseph	sleep
die	Mary	two
each	nail	watch
Eli	Naomi	which
Elijah	once	wise
family	poor	wood
found		word